How to Read Measurements

BY CATHERINE IPCIZADE

The Child's World®
childsworld.com

Published by The Child's World®
1980 Lookout Drive • Mankato, MN 56003-1705
800-599-READ • www.childsworld.com

Photographs ©: Shutterstock Images, cover (foreground), cover (background), 3, 7, 17, 18, 19, 23; iStockphoto, 5, 6, 13; Gregory Dean/Shutterstock Images, 9; Syda Productions/Shutterstock Images, 11; Adam Derewecki/Shutterstock Images, 12; Quang Ho/Shutterstock Images, 14 (left); Wathanyu Sowong/Shutterstock Images, 14 (right); Ann Worthy/Shutterstock Images, 16

ISBN 9781503823327
LCCN 2017944891

Printed in the United States of America
PA02360

ABOUT THE AUTHOR

Catherine Ipcizade is the author of more than 30 books for children. She writes fiction, nonfiction, and poetry for all age levels. She also teaches academic and creative writing to college students. She holds an MFA degree in Creative Writing.

Table of Contents

Measurements Matter

Joey wants to ride a roller coaster. The sign says he has to be 48 inches (122 cm) tall to ride. He needs to know his height. Joey could use a measuring tape.

Sophia likes to build objects using wood. She wants to build a birdhouse. Sophia needs to use a ruler.

Robin wants to bake a cake. She wants to make sure the cake recipe turns out just right. She needs to use measuring cups and measuring spoons.

People use measuring tools to make projects.

You might use measuring tools at school.

Knowing how to read measurements is important. Measurements are numbers that people use to organize objects. Measurements can also be used to help people understand objects. For example, measuring the weight of an object tells you if it is light or heavy.

Measurements can be used to make **standards**. For example, airplanes and elevators have weight standards. An airplane with too much weight onboard cannot fly. An elevator carrying too much weight cannot go up and down safely. A bridge that is not long or wide enough to cross is unusable. Measurements help people **calculate** and make decisions every day.

Airplanes and many other vehicles have weight standards.

Measuring Length

Measurements can be used for many different purposes. Measurements can help people build things or make projects. Important tools that might be needed for these purposes would be rulers, yardsticks, or measuring tapes. These tools measure length. For example, you might use these tools when building a tree house. The tree swing might need to be a certain distance from the tree. In order to build the swing, you would need to first measure and cut the materials.

A measuring tape can be used to measure long objects.

Projects usually come with instructions. The instructions might tell you that the rope for the swing should be exactly 3 feet (0.9 m) long. You would need a tool that would give you an exact measurement. You could use a yardstick. Yardsticks are like long rulers. They are exactly 3 feet (0.9 m) long. The yardstick would allow you to measure the rope exactly. Or you might choose to use a measuring tape instead. Measuring tapes are longer than rulers. Unlike rulers, they can bend. Many standard yardsticks and measuring tapes measure length in inches and in feet.

Rulers are also common measuring tools.

If you are building a swing, you would also need to measure wood for the seat. The seat might need to be 2 feet (0.6 m) long. You could use a ruler to measure the wood. Many standard rulers are 1 foot (0.3 m) long. Each foot is made up of 12 inches (30 cm).

American football fields are measured in yards.

There are two main measurement systems. In the United States, the Imperial System is used. In other parts of the world, the Metric System is used. Imperial **units** for length and distance include inches, feet, yards, and miles. Metric units for length and distance include millimeters, centimeters, meters, and kilometers.

Knowing which tools to use can be tricky. Short objects are often measured using rulers. Longer objects are often measured using yardsticks or measuring tapes. We use centimeters or inches to measure the length or width of small objects. We use feet or meters to measure longer objects, such as soccer fields. For distances, we use miles or kilometers.

Height can be measured with longer rulers or measuring tapes.

Length/Width

How It's Measured

Imperial
inches
feet
yards
miles

Metric
millimeters
centimeters
meters
kilometers

Conversions
1 foot = 12 inches
1 yard = 3 feet
1 mile = 1,760 yards
1 centimeter = 10 millimeters
1 meter = 100 centimeters
1 kilometer = 1,000 meters

Volume/Weight

How It's Measured

Imperial
fluid ounces   gallons
cups   ounces
pints   pounds
quarts

Metric
milliliters
liters
grams
kilograms

Conversions
1 cup = 8 fluid ounces
1 quart = 2 pints
1 gallon = 4 quarts
1 pound = 16 ounces
1 liter = 1,000 milliliters
1 kilogram = 1,000 grams

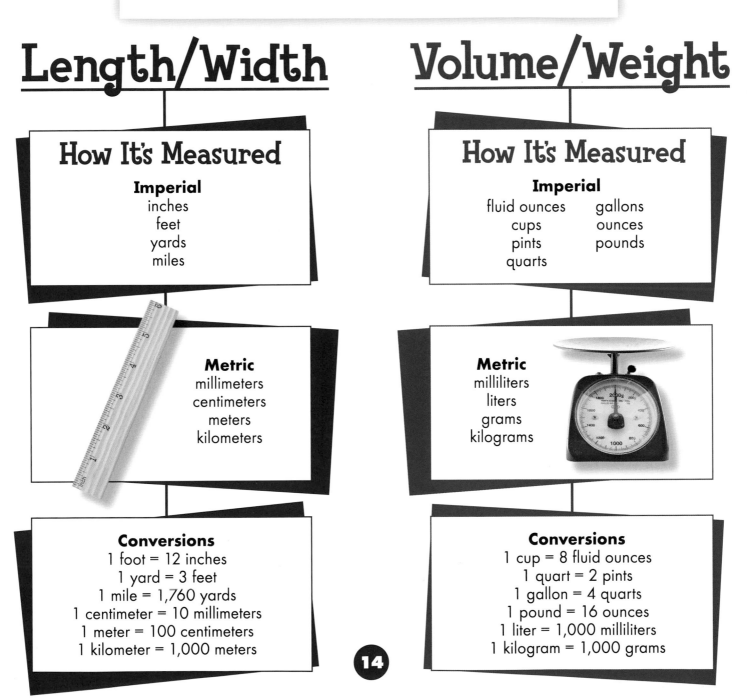

Measuring Volume and Weight

When people cook or bake, they use measuring tools. These tools can include measuring cups, measuring spoons, or a food scale. These tools measure the **volume** and weight of ingredients.

If you are making cookies, you would probably need flour, sugar, and baking powder. You could use a measuring cup or a measuring spoon to measure these ingredients. You would also probably need oil, milk, and vanilla. You could use a liquid measuring cup to measure these ingredients.

Liquid measuring cups measure the volume of a liquid. These cups have markings on the side. The markings measure liquids in both cups and fluid ounces. In the United States, people usually measure liquid in fluid ounces, cups, pints, quarts, or gallons. In countries that use the Metric System, people commonly use milliliters or liters.

Liquid measuring cups are used to measure volume.

Food scales can help people weigh food in grocery stores.

Some recipes might ask you to measure ingredients by their weight. For example, you might need to measure flour in ounces or grams. You could use a food scale to measure the weight of the flour. A food scale has a flat surface or a bowl where you put the ingredient. The scale measures the force of **gravity** on an object. This gives you its weight.

Larger scales can measure larger objects such as people. Larger objects are usually measured in pounds or kilograms. Common measurements for weight in the United States include ounces or pounds. Countries that use the Metric System commonly measure weight in grams or kilograms.

Another tool that measures volume is a graduated cylinder. A graduated cylinder might be used to measure liquids in a science experiment. Graduated cylinders have markings on the side. The markings usually measure liquids in milliliters.

You might use measurements for science experiments.

Measurements help people do many kinds of tasks. People use measurements to organize and understand objects. Now you are all set to use measurements!

1. Which tool measures volume?
    A. a yardstick
    B. a graduated cylinder
    C. a scale

2. What are the Imperial units for length and distance?

3. Which tool measures length?

    A. a measuring cup

    B. a ruler

    C. a scale

4. What does a scale measure?

GLOSSARY

calculate (KAL-kyoo-layt) To calculate is to work something out mathematically. Measurements help people calculate.

gravity (GRAV-uh-tee) Gravity is a force that pulls objects down toward the surface of the Earth. Weight is the force of gravity on an object.

standards (STAND-erdz) Standards are information set up as a rule or guide. Airplanes and elevators have weight standards.

units (YOO-nitz) Units are amounts that are used as standards for measurement. The United States uses Imperial units.

volume (VAHL-yoom) Volume is a measurement that describes how much liquid is in something. Liquid measuring cups and graduated cylinders help people measure volume.

TO LEARN MORE

In the Library

Pistoia, Sara, and Piper Whelan. *Measurements.* New York, NY: AV2 by Weigl, 2017.

Vogel, Julia. *Measuring Volume.* Mankato, MN: The Child's World, 2013.

On the Web

Visit our Web site for links about how to read measurements:
childsworld.com/links

Note to Parents, Teachers, and Librarians: We routinely verify our Web links to make sure they are safe and active sites. So encourage your readers to check them out!

INDEX

ANSWER KEY

1. **Which tool measures volume?** B. a graduated cylinder

2. **What are the Imperial units for length and distance?** The Imperial units for length and distance are inches, feet, yards, and miles.

3. **Which tool measures length?** B. a ruler

4. **What does a scale measure?** A scale measures the force of gravity on an object, which gives you the object's weight.